Classic

LOVE POEMS

ILLUSTRATED BY
LAWRENCE MYNOTT

CHANCELLOR
PRESS

This volume first published in Great Britain in 1988 by
Chancellor Press
59 Grosvenor Street
London W1

Illustrated by Lawrence Maynott

ISBN 1 85152 059 7

Printed in Hong Kong

CONTENTS

CELEBRATION

Love's not Time's fool, though rosy lips and cheeks
Within his bending sickle's compass come;
Love alters not with his brief hours and weeks,
But bears it out even to the edge of doom.
If this be error, and upon me proved,
I never writ, nor no man ever loved.

William Shakespeare

The Bargain

My true love hath my heart, and I have his,
By just exchange, one for the other given.
I hold his dear, and mine he cannot miss,
There never was a better bargain driven.
His heart in me keeps me and him in one,
My heart in him his thoughts and senses guides;
He loves my heart, for once it was his own,
I cherish his, because in me it bides.
His heart his wound receivèd from my sight,
My heart was wounded with his wounded heart;
For as from me on him his hurt did light,
So still methought in me his hurt did smart.
Both equal hurt, in this change sought our bliss:
My true love hath my heart and I have his.

Sir Philip Sidney

Delight in Disorder

A sweet disorder in the dress
Kindles in clothes a wantonness:
A lawn about the shoulders thrown
Into a fine distraction:
An erring lace, which here and there,
Enthrals the crimson stomacher:
A cuff neglectful, and thereby
Ribbands to flow confusedly:
A winning wave (deserving note)
In the tempestuous petticoat:
A careless shoe-string, in whose tie
I see a wild civility:
Do more bewitch me, than when Art
Is too precise in every part!

Robert Herrick

Sonnet 18

Shall I compare thee to a summer's day?
Thou art more lovely and more temperate:
Rough winds do shake the darling buds of May,
And summer's lease hath all too short a date:
Sometime too hot the eye of heaven shines,
And often is his gold complexion dimmed;
And every fair from fair sometime declines,
By chance, or nature's changing course untrimmed;
But thy eternal summer shall not fade,
Nor lose possession of that fair thou owest,
Nor shall death brag thou wanderest in his shade,
When in eternal lines to time thou growest;
So long as men can breathe, or eyes can see,
So long lives this, and this gives life to thee.

William Shakespeare

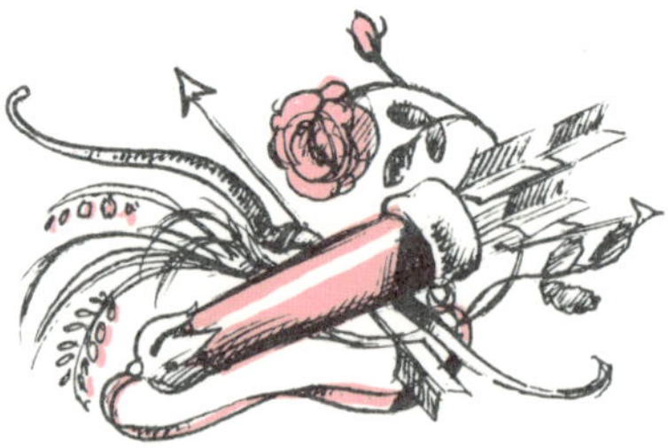

The Good Morrow

I wonder by my troth, what thou, and I
Did, till we lov'd? were we not wean'd till then?
But suck'd on country pleasures, childishly?
Or snorted we in the seven sleepers den?
T'was so; But this, all pleasures fancies be.
If ever any beauty I did see,
Which I desir'd, and got, t'was but a dreame of thee.

And now good morrow to our waking soules,
Which watch not one another out of feare;
For love, all love of other sights controles,
And makes one little roome, an every where.
Let sea discoverers to new worlds have gone,
Let maps to other, worlds on worlds have shown,
Let us possess one world, each hath one, and is one.

My face in thine eye, thine in mine appeares,
And true plain hearts do in the faces rest,
Where can we finde two better hemispheres
Without sharpe North, without declining West?
What ever dies, was not mixt equally;
If our two loves be one, or, thou and I
Love so alike, that none do slacken, none can die.

John Donne

To Celia

Drinke to me, onely, with thine eyes,
And I will pledge with mine;
Or leave a kisse but in the cup,
And Ile not looke for wine.
The thirst, that from the soule doth rise,
Doth aske a drinke divine:
But might I of Jove's Nectar *sup,*
I would not change for thine.
I sent thee, late, a rosie wreath,
Not so much honoring thee,
As giving it a hope, that there
It could not withered bee.
But thou thereon did'st onely breath,
And sent'st it back to mee:
Since when it growes, and smells, I sweare,
Not of it selfe, but thee.

Ben Jonson

First Love

I ne'er was struck before that hour
With love so sudden and so sweet.
Her face it bloomed like a sweet flower
And stole my heart away complete.
My face turned pale as deadly pale,
My legs refused to walk away,
And when she looked 'what could I ail?'
My life and all seemed turned to clay.

And then my blood rushed to my face
And took my sight away.
The trees and bushes round the place
Seemed midnight at noonday.
I could not see a single thing,
Words from my eyes did start;
They spoke as chords do from the string
And blood burnt round my heart.

Are flowers the winter's choice?
Is love's bed always snow?
She seemed to hear my silent voice
And love's appeal to know.
I never saw so sweet a face
As that I stood before:
My heart has left its dwelling-place
And can return no more.

John Clare

'She walks in beauty, like the night'

She walks in beauty, like the night
Of cloudless climes and starry skies;
And all that's best of dark and bright
Meet in her aspect and her eyes:
Thus mellowed to that tender light
Which heaven to gaudy day denies.

One shade the more, one ray the less,
Had half impaired the nameless grace
Which waves in every raven tress,
Or softly lightens o'er her face;
Where thoughts serenely sweet express
How pure, how dear their dwelling-place.

And on that cheek, and o'er that brow,
So soft, so calm, yet eloquent,
The smiles that win, the tints that glow,
But tell of days in goodness spent,
A mind at peace with all below,
A heart whose love is innocent.

Lord Byron

'How do I love thee?
Let me count the ways'

How do I love thee? Let me count the ways.
I love thee to the depth and breadth and height
My soul can reach, when feeling out of sight
For the ends of Being and ideal Grace.
I love thee to the level of everyday's
Most quiet need, by sun and candle light.
I love thee freely, as men strive for Right;
I love thee purely, as they turn from Praise.
I love thee with the passion put to use
In my old griefs, and with my childhood's faith.
I love thee with a love I seemed to lose
With my lost saints—I love thee with the breath,
Smiles, tears, of all my life!—and, if God choose,
I shall but love thee better after death.

Elizabeth Barrett Browning

Dear Dark Head

Put your head, darling, darling, darling,
Your darling black head my heart above;
Oh, mouth of honey with the thyme for fragrance,
Who with heart in his breast could deny you
love?

Oh, many and many a young girl for me is pining,
Letting her locks of gold to the cold wind free,
For me, the foremost of our gay young fellows;
But I'd leave a hundred, pure love, for thee!

Then put your head, darling, darling, darling,
Your darling black head my heart above;
Oh, mouth of honey with the thyme for fragrance,
Who with heart in his breast could deny you
love?

Anon.
Translated from the Gaelic
by Sir Samuel Ferguson

LAMENTATION

Western winde, when will thou blow,
The smalle raine down can raine?
Christ if my love were in my armes,
And I in my bed againe.

Anon.

Remembrance

They flee from me, that sometime did me seek
With naked foot, stalking in my chamber.
I have seen them gentle, tame, and meek,
That now are wild, and do not remember
That sometime they put themselves in danger
To take bread at my hand; and now they range
Busily seeking with a continual change.

Thanked be fortune it hath been otherwise
Twenty times better; but once, in special,
In thin array, after a pleasant guise,
When her loose gown from her shoulders did fall,
And she me caught in her arms long and small,
Therewith all sweetly did me kiss
And softly said, 'Dear heart, how like you this?'

It was no dream; I lay broad waking:
But all is turned, thorough my gentleness,
Into a strange fashion of forsaking;
And I have leave to go of her goodness,
And she also to use newfangleness.
But since that I so kindly am served,
I would fain know what she hath deserved.

Sir Thomas Wyatt

'One day I wrote her name upon the strand'

One day I wrote her name upon the strand,
But came the waves and washed it away:
Agayne I wrote it with a second hand,
But came the tyde, and made my paynes his pray.
'Vayne man,' sayd she, 'that doest in vaine assay,
A mortall thing so to immortalize,
For I my selve shall lyke to this decay,
And eek my name bee wyped out lykewize.'
'Not so,' quod I, 'let baser things devize
To dy in dust, but you shall live by fame:
My verse your vertues rare shall eternize,
And in the hevens wryte your glorious name.
Where whenas death shall all the world subdew,
Our love shall live, and later life renew.'

Edmund Spenser

Sonnet 129

The expense of spirit in a waste of shame
Is lust in action; and till action, lust
Is perjured, murderous, bloody, full of blame,
Savage, extreme, rude, cruel, not to trust;
Enjoyed, no sooner but despised straight;
Past reason hunted; and no sooner had,
Past reason hated, as a swallowed bait,
On purpose laid to make the taker mad:
Mad in pursuit, and in possession so;
Had, having, and in quest to have, extreme;
A bliss in proof, and proved, a very woe;
Before, a joy proposed; behind, a dream.
All this the world well knows; yet none knows well
To shun the heaven that leads men to this hell.

William Shakespeare

The Shower of Blossoms

Love in a shower of blossoms came
Down, and half drown'd me with the same:
The blooms that fell were white and red;
But with such sweets commingléd
As whether—this I cannot tell—
My sight was pleas'd more, or my smell:
But true it was, as I roll'd there,
Without a thought of hurt or fear,
Love turn'd himself into a bee,
And with his javelin wounded me:
From which mishaps this use I make
Where most sweets are, there lies a snake;
Kisses and favours are sweet things;
But those have thorns and these have stings.

Robert Herrick

To Mary: I sleep with thee, and wake with thee

I sleep with thee, and wake with thee,
And yet thou art not there;
I fill my arms with thoughts of thee,
And press the common air.
Thy eyes are gazing upon mine,
When thou art out of sight;
My lips are always touching thine,
At morning, noon, and night.

I think and speak of other things
To keep my mind at rest:
But still to thee my memory clings
Like love in woman's breast.
I hide it from the world's wide eye,
And think and speak contrary;
But soft the wind comes from the sky,
And whispers tales of Mary.

The night wind whispers in my ear,
The moon shines in my face;
A burden still of chilling fear
I find in every place.
The breeze is whispering in the bush,
And the dews fall from the tree,
All sighing on, and will not hush,
Some pleasant tales of thee.

John Clare

'So, we'll go no more a-roving'

So, we'll go no more a-roving
So late into the night,
Though the heart be still as loving,
And the moon be still as bright.

For the sword outwears its sheath,
And the soul wears out the breast,
And the heart must pause to breathe,
And love itself have rest.

Though the night was made for loving,
And the day returns too soon,
Yet we'll go no more a-roving
By the light of the moon.

Lord Byron

La Belle Dame Sans Merci

'O what can ail thee, knight-at-arms,
Alone and palely loitering?
The sedge is wither'd from the lake,
And no birds sing.

O what can ail thee, knight-at-arms,
So haggard and so woe-begone?
The squirrel's granary is full,
And the harvest's done.

I see a lily on thy brow
With anguish moist and fever dew;
And on thy cheek a fading rose
Fast withereth too.'

'I met a lady in the meads,
Full beautiful – a faery's child,
Her hair was long, her foot was light,
And her eyes were wild.

I made a garland for her head,
And bracelets too, and fragrant zone;
She look'd at me as she did love,
And made sweet moan.

I set her on my pacing steed
And nothing else saw all day long,
For sideways would she lean, and sing
A faery's song.

She found me roots of relish sweet,
And honey wild and manna dew,
And sure in language strange she said,
"I love thee true!"

She took me to her elfin grot,
And there she wept and sigh'd full sore;
And there I shut her wild, wild eyes
With kisses four.

And there she lullèd me asleep,
And there I dream'd – Ah! woe betide!
The latest dream I ever dream'd
On the cold hill's side.

I saw pale kings and princes too,
Pale warriors, death-pale were they all;
Who cried – "La belle Dame sans Merci
Hath thee in thrall!"

I saw their starved lips in the gloam
With horrid warning gapèd wide,
And I awoke and found me here
On the cold hill's side.

And this is why I sojourn here
Alone and palely loitering,
Though the sedge is wither'd from the lake,
And no birds sing.'

John Keats

'Are you the new person drawn toward me?'

Are you the new person drawn toward me?
To begin with, take warning, I am surely far
different from what you suppose;
Do you suppose you will find in me your ideal?
Do you think it so easy to have me become your
lover?
Do you think the friendship of me would be
unalloy'd satisfaction?
Do you think I am trusty and faithful?
Do you see no further than this facade, this smooth
and tolerant manner of me?
Do you suppose yourself advancing on real ground
toward a real heroic man?
Have you no thought, O dreamer, that it may be all
maya, illusion?

Walt Whitman

A Broken Appointment

You did not come,
And marching Time drew on, and wore me numb, —
Yet less for loss of your dear presence there
Than that I thus found lacking in your make
That high compassion which can overbear
Reluctance for pure loving kindness' sake
Grieved I, when, as the hope-hour stroked its sum,
You did not come.

You love not me,
And love alone can lend you loyalty;
– I know and knew it. But, unto the store
Of human deeds divine in all but name,
Was it not worth a little hour or more
To add yet this: Once you, a woman, came
To soothe a time-torn man; even though it be
You love not me?

Thomas Hardy

When I was one-and-twenty

When I was one-and-twenty
I heard a wise man say,
'Give crowns and pounds and guineas
But not your heart away;
Give pearls away and rubies
But keep your fancy free.'
But I was one-and-twenty,
No use to talk to me.

When I was one-and-twenty
I heard him say again,
'The heart out of the bosom
Was never given in vain;
'Tis paid with sighs a-plenty
And sold for endless rue.'
And I am two-and-twenty,
And oh, 'tis true, 'tis true.

A. E. Housman

EXPECTATION

My Love in her attire doth show her wit,
It doth so well become her;
For every season she hath dressings fit,
For Winter, Spring, and Summer.
No beauty she doth miss
When all her robes are on:
But Beauty's self she is
When all her robes are gone.

Anon.

Kissing

Come hither, womankind and all their worth,
Give me thy kisses as I call them forth.
Give me the billing kiss, that of the dove,
A kiss of love;
The melting kiss, a kiss that doth consume
To a perfume;
The extract kiss, of every sweet a part,
A kiss of art;
The kiss which ever stirs some new delight,
A kiss of might;
The twaching smacking kiss, and when you cease,
A kiss of peace;
The music kiss, crochet-and-quaver time;
The kiss of rhyme;
The kiss of eloquence, which doth belong
Unto the tongue;
The kiss of all the sciences in one,
The Kiss alone.
So, 'tis enough.

Edward Herbert

Up Tailes All

Begin with a kisse,
Go on too with this:
And thus, thus, thus let us smother
Our lips for a while,
But let's not beguile
Our hope of one for the other.

This play, be assur'd,
Long enough has endur'd,
Since more and more is exacted;
For love he doth call
For his Uptailes all;
And that's the part to be acted.

Robert Herrick

The Passionate Shepherd to His Love

Come live with me, and be my love,
And we will all the pleasures prove
That valleys, groves, hills and fields,
Woods, or steepy mountain yields.

And we will sit upon the rocks,
Seeing the shepherds feed their flocks
By shallow rivers, to whose falls
Melodious birds sing madrigals.

And I will make thee beds of roses,
And a thousand fragrant posies;
A cap of flowers, and a kirtle,
Embroider'd all with leaves of myrtle.

A gown made of the finest wool,
Which from our pretty lambs we pull;
Fair lined slippers for the cold,
With buckles of the purest gold.

A belt of straw and ivy buds,
With coral clasps and amber studs,
An if these pleasures may thee move,
Come live with me, and be my love.

The shepherd swains shall dance and sing
For thy delight each May-morning:
If these delights thy mind may move,
Then live with me, and be my love.

Christopher Marlowe

The Nymph's Reply to the Shepherd

If all the world and love were young,
And truth in every shepherd's tongue,
These pretty pleasures might me move
To live with thee and be thy love.

Time drives the flocks from field to fold,
When rivers rage and rocks grow cold,
And Philomel becometh dumb;
The rest complains of cares to come.

The flowers do fade, and wanton fields
To wayward winter reckoning yields;
A honey tongue, a heart of gall,
Is fancy's spring, but sorrow's fall.

Thy gowns, thy shoes, thy beds of roses,
Thy cap, thy kirtle, and thy posies
Soon break, soon wither, soon forgotten,
In folly ripe, in reason rotten.

Thy belt of straw and ivy buds,
Thy coral clasps and amber studs,
All these in me no means can move
To come to thee and be thy love.

But could youth last and love still breed,
Had joys no date nor age no need,
Then these delights my mind might move
To live with thee and be thy love.

Sir Walter Raleigh

Song

The lark now leaves his wat'ry nest,
And climbing, shakes his dewy wings;
He takes this window for the east,
And to implore your light, he sings,
Awake, awake, the morn will never rise,
Till she can dress her beauty at your eyes.

The merchant bows unto the seaman's star,
The ploughman from the sun his season takes;
But still the lover wonders what they are,
Who look for day before his mistress wakes.
Awake, awake, break through your veils of lawn,
Then draw your curtains, and begin the dawn.

Sir John Davenant

A Paraphrase

The beauty that must me delight,
Must have a skin and teeth snow white:
Black arched brows, black sprightly eyes,
And a black beauty 'twixt her thighs;
Soft blushing cheeks, a person tall,
Long hair, long hands, and fingers small;
Short teeth; and feet that little are,
Dilated brows, and haunches fair;
Fine silken hair, lips full and red,
Small nose, with little breast and head:
All these in one, and that one kind
Would make a mistress to my mind.

Charles Cotton

An Argument

I've oft been told by learned friars,
That wishing and the crime are one,
And Heaven punishes desires
As much as if the deed were done.

If wishing damns us, you and I
Are damned to all our heart's content;
Come, then, at least we may enjoy
Some pleasure for our punishment!

Thomas Moore

Give All To Love

Give all to love;
Obey thy heart;
Friends, kindred, days,
Estate, good-fame,
Plans, credit and the Muse, —
Nothing refuse.

'Tis a brave master;
Let it have scope:
Follow it utterly,
Hope beyond hope:
High and more high
It dives into noon,
With wing unspent,
Untold intent;
But it is a god,
Knows its own path
And the outlets of the sky.

It was never for the mean;
It requireth courage stout.
Souls above doubt,
Valor unbending,
It will reward, —
They shall return
More than they were,
And ever ascending.

Leave all for love;
Yet, hear me, yet,
One word more thy heart behoved,
One pulse more of firm endeavor, —
Keep thee to-day,
To-morrow, forever,
Free as an Arab
Of thy beloved.

Cling with life to the maid;
But when the surprise,
First vague shadow of surmise
Flits across her bosom young,
Of a joy apart from thee,
Free be she, fancy-free;
Nor thou detain her vesture's hem,
Nor the palest rose she flung
From her summer diadem.

Though thou loved her as thyself,
As a self of purer clay,
Though her parting dims the day,
Stealing grace from all alive;
Heartily know,
When half-gods go,
The gods arrive.

Ralph Waldo Emerson

The Jilted Nymph

I'm jilted, forsaken, outwitted;
Yet think not I'll whimper or brawl –
The lass is alone to be pitied
Who ne'er has been courted at all:
Never by great or small,
Woo'd or jilted at all;
Oh, how unhappy's the lass
Who has never been courted at all!

What though at my heart he has tilted,
What though I have met with a fall?
Better be courted and jilted
Than never be courted at all.
Woo'd and jilted and all,
Still I will dance at the ball;
And waltz and quadrille
With light heart and heel,
With proper young men and tall.

Thomas Campbell

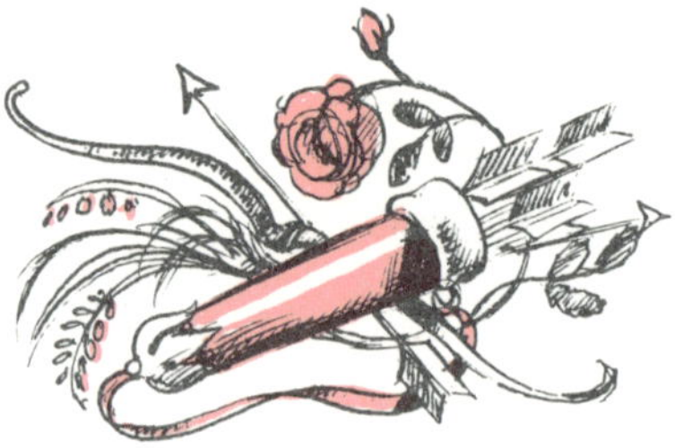

SEPARATION

Stay; O sweet, and do not rise,
The light that shines comes from thine eyes;
The day breaks not, it is my heart,
Because that you and I must part.
Stay, or else my joys will die,
And perish in their infancy.

Anon.

'Since there's no help, come let us kiss and part'

Since there's no help, come let us kiss and part –
Nay, I have done, you get no more of me;
And I am glad, yea, glad with all my heart,
That thus so cleanly I myself can free.
Shake hands for ever, cancel all our vows,
And when we meet at any time again,
Be it not seen in either of our brows
That we one jot of former love retain.
Now at the last gasp of Love's latest breath,
When, his pulse failing, Passion speechless lies,
When Faith is kneeling by his bed of death,
And Innocence is closing up his eyes,
– Now if thou would'st, when all have given him over,
From death to life thou might'st him yet recover.

Michael Drayton

Sonnet 87

Farewell! thou art too dear for my possessing,
And like enough thou know'st thy estimate:
The charter of thy worth gives thee releasing;
My bonds in thee are all determinate.
For how do I hold thee but by thy granting?
And for that riches where is my deserving?
The cause of this fair gift in me is wanting,
And so my patent back again is swerving.
Thyself thou gav'st, thy own worth then not knowing,
Or me, to whom thou gav'st it, else mistaking;
So thy great gift, upon misprision growing,
Comes home again, on better judgement making.
Thus have I had thee, as a dream doth flatter,
In sleep a king, but, waking, no such matter.

William Shakespeare

Song

Sweetest love, I do not go
For weariness of thee,
Nor in hope the world can show
A fitter love for me;
But since that I
Must die at last, 'tis best
To use myself in jest
Thus by fained deaths to die.

Yesternight the sun went hence,
And yet is here today,
He hath no desire nor sense,
Nor half so short a way:
Then fear not me,
But believe that I shall make
Speedier journeys, since I take
More wings and spurs than he.

O how feeble is man's power,
That if good fortune fall,
Cannot add another hour,
Nor a lost hour recall!
But come bad chance,
And we join to it our strength,
And we teach it art and length,
Itself o'er us to advance.

When thou sigh'st, thou sigh'st not wind,
But sigh'st my soul away,
When thou weep'st, unkindly kind,
My life's blood doth decay.
It cannot be
That thou lov'st me, as thou sayst,
If in thine my life thou waste,
Thou art the best of me.

Let not thy divining heart
Forethink me any ill,
Destiny may take thy part,
And may thy fears fulfil.
But think that we
Are but turned aside to sleep;
They who one another keep
Alive, ne'er parted be.

John Donne

A Red, Red Rose

O my Luve's like a red, red rose
That's newly sprung in June:
O my Luve's like the melodie
That's sweetly play'd in tune!

As fair art thou, my bonnie lass,
So deep in luve am I:
And I will luve thee still, my dear,
Till a' the seas gang dry:

Till a' the seas gang dry, my dear,
And the rocks melt wi' the sun;
I will luve thee still, my dear,
While the sands o' life shall run.

And fare thee weel, my only Luve,
And fare thee weel a while!
And I will come again, my Luve,
Tho' it were ten thousand mile.

Robert Burns

'When we two parted'

When we two parted
In silence and tears,
Half broken-hearted,
To sever for years,
Pale grew thy cheek and cold,
Colder thy kiss;
Truly that hour foretold
Sorrow to this!

The dew of the morning
Sunk chill on my brow;
It felt like the warning
Of what I feel now.
Thy vows are all broken,
And light is thy fame:
I hear thy name spoken
And share in its shame.

They name thee before me,
A knell to mine ear;
A shudder comes o'er me –
Why wert thou so dear?
They know not I knew thee
Who knew thee too well:
Long, long shall I rue thee
Too deeply to tell.

In secret we met:
In silence I grieve
That thy heart could forget,
Thy spirit deceive.
If I should meet thee
After long years,
How should I greet thee? –
With silence and tears.

Lord Byron

'I will not let thee go'

I will not let thee go.
Ends all our month-long love in this?
Can it be summed up so,
Quit in a single kiss?
I will not let thee go.

I will not let thee go.
If thy words' breath could scare thy deeds,
As the soft south can blow
And toss the feathered seeds,
Then might I let thee go.

I will not let thee go.
Had not the great sun seen, I might;
Or were he reckoned slow
To bring the false to light,
Then might I let thee go.

I will not let thee go.
The stars that crowd the summer skies
Have watched us so below
With all their million eyes,
I dare not let thee go.

I will not let thee go.
Have we not chid the changeful moon,
Now rising late and now
Because she set too soon,
And shall I let thee go?

I will not let thee go.
Have not the young flowers been content,
Plucked ere their buds could blow,
To seal our sacrament?
I cannot let thee go.

I will not let thee go.
I hold thee by too many bands:
Thou sayest farewell, and lo!
I have thee by the hands,
And will not let thee go.

Robert Bridges

An Interlude

I remember the way we parted,
The day and the way we met;
You hoped we were both broken-hearted,
And knew we should both forget.

And the best and the worst of this is
That neither is most to blame,
If you have forgotten my kisses,
And I have forgotten your name.

Algernon Charles Swinburne

A Farewell

With all my will, but much against my heart,
We two now part.
My Very Dear,
Our solace is, the sad road lies so clear.
It needs no art,
With faint, averted feet
And many a tear,
In our opposed paths to persevere.
Go thou to East, I West.
We will not say
There's any hope, it is so far away.
But, O, my Best,
When the one darling of our widowhead,
The nursling Grief,
Is dead,
And no dews blur our eyes
To see the peach-bloom come in evening skies,
Perchance we may,
Where now this night is day,
And even through faith of still averted feet,
Making full circle of our banishment,
Amazed meet;
The bitter journey to the bourne so sweet
Seasoning the termless feast of our content
With tears of recognition never dry.

Coventry Patmore

CONSUMMATION

What is it men in women do require?
The lineaments of Gratified Desire.
What is it women do in men require?
The lineaments of Gratified Desire.

William Blake

'Coming to kiss her lips'

Coming to kiss her lips, (such grace I found)
Me seemed I smelt a garden of sweet flowers:
That dainty odours from them threw around
For damsels fit to deck their lovers' bowers.
Her lips did smell like unto gillyflowers,
Her ruddy cheeks like unto roses red:
Her snowy brows like budded bellamoures,
Her lovely eyes like pinks but newly spread.
Her goodly bosom like a strawberry bed,
Her neck like to a bunch of colombines:
Her breast like lillies, ere their leaves be shed,
Her nipples like young blossomed jessamines.
Such fragrant flowers do give most odorous smell,
But her sweet odour did them all excell.

Edmund Spenser

Corinnae Concubitus

In summer's heat and mid-time of the day
To rest my limbs upon a bed I lay,
One window shut, the other open stood,
Which gave such light as twinkles in a wood,
Like twilight glimpse at setting of the sun
Or night being past, and yet not day begun.
Such light to shamefaced maidens must be shown,
Where they may sport, and seem to be unknown.
Then came Corinna in a long loose gown,
Her white neck hid with tresses hanging down:
Resembling fair Semiramis going to bed
Or Lais of a thousand wooers sped.
I snatched her gown, being thin, the harm was small,
Yet strived she to be covered therewithal.
And striving thus as one that would be cast,
Betrayed herself, and yielded at the last.
Stark naked as she stood before mine eye,
Not one wen in her body could I spy.
What arms and shoulders did I touch and see,
How apt her breasts were to be pressed by me!
How smooth a belly under her waist saw I!
How large a leg, and what a lusty thigh!
To leave the rest, all liked me passing well,
I clinged her naked body, down she fell,
Judge you the rest: being tired she bad me kiss,
Jove send me more such afternoons as this.

Christopher Marlowe

To His Mistress Going To Bed

Come, Madam, come, all rest my powers defy,
Until I labour, I in labour lie.
The foe oft-times, having the foe in sight,
Is tired with standing, though they never fight.
Off with that girdle, like heaven's zone glistering
But a far fairer world encompassing.
Unpin that spangled breast-plate, which you wear
That th'eyes of busy fools may be stopped there:
Unlace yourself, for that harmonious chime
Tells me from you that now 'tis your bed time.
Off with that happy busk, whom I envy
That still can be, and still can stand so nigh.
Your gown's going off such beauteous state reveals
As when from flowery meads th'hills shadow steals.
Off with your wiry coronet and show
The hairy diadem which on you doth grow.
Off with those shoes: and then safely tread
In this love's hallowed temple, this soft bed.
In such white robes heaven's angels used to be
Received by men; thou Angel bring'st with thee
A heaven like Mahomet's Paradise; and though
Ill spirits walk in white, we easily know
By this these Angels from an evil sprite:
They set our hairs, but these the flesh upright.
    Licence my roving hands, and let them go
Behind, before, above, between, below.

Oh my America, my new found land,
My kingdom, safeliest when with one man manned,
My mine of precious stones, my Empery,
How blessed am I in this discovering thee.
To enter in these bonds is to be free,
Then where my hand is set my seal shall be.
Full nakedness, all joys are due to thee.
As souls unbodied, bodies unclothed must be
To taste whole joys. Gems which you women use
Are as Atlanta's balls, cast in men's views,
That when a fool's eye lighteth on a gem
His earthly soul may covet theirs not them.
Like pictures, or like books' gay coverings made
For laymen, are all women thus arrayed;
Themselves are mystic books, which only we
Whom their imputed grace will dignify
Must see revealed. Then since I may know,
As liberally as to a midwife show
Thyself; cast all, yea this white linen hence.
Here is no penance, much less innocence.
To teach thee, I am naked first: Why then
What need'st thou have more covering than a man.

John Donne

'I gently touched her hand'

I gently touched her hand: she gave
A look that did my soul enslave;
I pressed her rebel lips in vain:
They rose up to be pressed again.
Thus happy, I no farther meant,
Than to be pleased and innocent.

On her soft breasts my hand I laid,
And a quick, light impression made;
They with a kindly warmth did glow,
And swelled, and seemed to overflow.
Yet, trust me, I no farther meant,
Than to be pleased and innocent.

On her eyes my eyes did stay:
O'er her smooth limbs my hands did stray;
Each sense was ravished with delight,
And my soul stood prepared for flight.
Blame me not if at last I meant
More to be pleased than innocent.

Anon.

Ruth

She stood breast high amid the corn,
Clasped by the golden light of morn,
Like the sweetheart of the sun,
Who many a glowing kiss had won.

On her cheek an autumn flush,
Deeply ripened; – such a blush
In the midst of brown was born,
Like red poppies grown with corn.

Round her eyes her tresses fell,
Which were blackest none could tell,
But long lashes veiled a light,
That had else been all too bright.

And her hat, with shady brim,
Made her tressy forehead dim; –
Thus she stood amid the stooks,
Praising God with sweetest looks: –

Sure, I said, heaven did not mean,
Where I reap thou shouldst but glean,
Lay thy sheaf adown and come,
Share my harvest and my home.

Thomas Hood

'First time he kissed me, he but only kissed'

First time he kissed me, he but only kissed
The fingers of this hand wherewith I write;
And ever since, it grew more clean and white,
Slow to world-greetings, quick with its 'Oh, list,'
When the angels speak. A ring of amethyst
I could not wear here, plainer to my sight,
Than that first kiss. The second passed in height
The first, and sought the forehead, and half missed,
Half falling on the hair. O beyond meed!
That was the chrism of love, which love's own crown,
With sanctifying sweetness, did precede.
The third upon my lips was folded down
In perfect, purple state; since when, indeed,
I have been proud and said, 'My love, my own.'

Elizabeth Barrett Browning

'When I heard at the close of the day'

When I heard at the close of the day how my name
had been receiv'd with plaudits in the capitol, still
it was not a happy night for me that follow'd,
And else when I carous'd, or when my plans were
accomplish'd, still I was not happy,
But the day when I rose at dawn from the bed of
perfect health, refresh'd, singing, inhaling the
ripe breath of autumn,
When I saw the full moon in the west grow pale and
disappear in the morning light,
When I wander'd alone over the beach, and
undressing bathed, laughing with the cool waters,
and saw the sun rise,
And when I thought how my dear friend my lover
was on his way coming, O then I was happy,
O then each breath tasted sweeter, and all that day
my food nourish'd me more, and the beautiful day
pass'd well,
And the next came with equal joy, and with the
next at evening came my friend,
And that night while all was still I heard the waters
roll slowly continually up the shores,
I heard the hissing rustle of the liquid and sands as
directed to me whispering to congratulate me,
For the one I love most lay sleeping by me under the
same cover in the cool night,
In the stillness in the autumn moonbeams his face
was inclined toward me,
And his arm lay lightly around my breast—and that
night I was happy.

Walt Whitman

Love and Sleep

Lying asleep between the strokes of night
I saw my love lean over my sad bed,
Pale as the duskiest lily's leaf or head,
Smooth-skinned and dark, with bare throat made to bite,
Too wan for blushing and too warm for white,
But perfect-coloured without white or red.
And her lips opened amorously, and said –
I wist not what, saving one word – Delight.

And all her face was honey to my mouth,
And all her body pasture to mine eyes;
The long lithe arms and hotter hands than fire,
The quivering flanks, hair smelling of the south,
The bright light feet, the splendid supple thighs
And glittering eyelids of my soul's desire.

Algernon Charles Swinburne

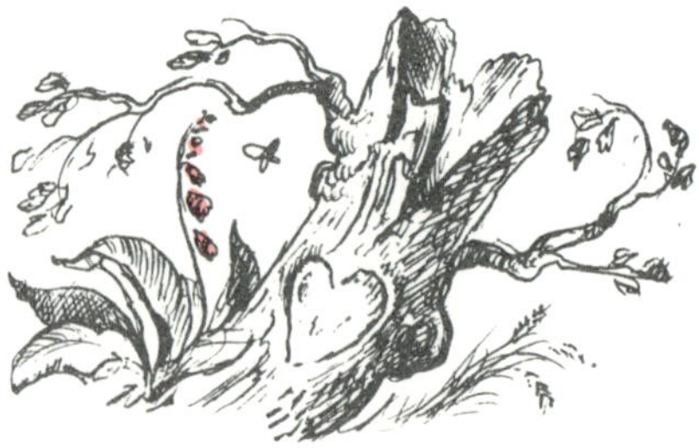

FRUSTRATION

She who is always in my thoughts prefers
Another man, and does not think of me.
Yet he seeks for another's love, not hers;
And some poor girl is grieving for my sake.
Why then, the devil take
Both her and him; and love; and her; and me.

Anon.

'Dear, why make you more of a dog than me?'

Dear, why make you more of a dog than me?
If he do love, I burn, I burn in love:
If he wait well, I never thence would move:
If he be fair, yet but a dog can be.
Little he is, so little worth is he;
He barks, my songs thine own voice oft doth prove:
Bidd'n, perhaps he fetcheth thee a glove,
But I unbid, fetch even my soul to thee.
Yet while I languish, him that bosom clips,
That lap doth lap, nay lets, in spite of spite,
This sour-breath'd mate taste of those sugar'd lips.
Alas, if you grant only such delight
To witless things, then Love I hope (since wit
Becomes a clog) will soon ease me of it.

Sir Philip Sidney

The Triple Fool

I am two fools, I know,
For loving, and for saying so
In whining poetry;
But where's that wise man, that would not be I,
If she would not deny?
Then as th'earth's inward narrow crooked lanes
Do purge sea water's fretful salt away,
I thought, if I could draw my pains
Through rhyme's vexations, I should them allay,
Grief brought to numbers cannot be so fierce,
For, he tames it, that fetters it in verse.

But when I have done so,
Some man, his art and voice to show,
Doth set and sing my pain,
And, by delighting many, frees again
Grief, which verse did restrain.

John Donne

To the Virgins, to Make Much of Time

Gather ye rosebuds while ye may,
Old Time is still a-flying:
And this same flower that smiles to-day
To-morrow will be dying.

The glorious lamp of heaven, the sun,
The higher he's a-getting,
The sooner will his race be run,
And nearer he's to setting.

That age is best which is the first,
When youth and blood are warmer;
But being spent, the worse, and worst
Times still succeed the former.

Then be not coy, but use your time,
And while ye may, go marry:
For having lost but once your prime,
You may for ever tarry.

Robert Herrick

To My Inconstant Mistress

When thou, poor excommunicate
From all the joys of love, shalt see
The full reward and glorious fate
Which my strong faith shall purchase me,
Then curse thine own inconstancy.

A fairer hand than thine shall cure
That heart, which thy false oaths did wound;
And to my soul a soul more pure
Than thine shall by Love's hand be bound,
And both with equal glory crown'd.

Then shalt thou weep, entreat, complain
To Love, as I did once to thee;
When all thy tears shall be as vain
As mine were then, for thou shalt be
Damn'd for thy false apostacy.

Thomas Carew

The Constant Lover

Out upon it, I have loved
Three whole days together!
And am like to love three more,
If it hold fair weather.

Time shall moult away his wings
Ere he shall discover
In the whole wide world again
Such a constant lover.

But a pox upon't, no praise
There is due at all to me:
Love with me had made no stay,
Had it any been but she.

Had it any been but she,
And that very very face,
There had been at least ere this
A dozen dozen in her place.

Sir John Suckling

Why So Pale And Wan

Why so pale and wan, fond lover?
Prithee, why so pale?
Will, when looking well can't move her,
Looking ill prevail?
Prithee, why so pale?

Why so dull and mute, young sinner?
Prithee, why so mute?
Will, when speaking well can't win her,
Saying nothing do't?
Prithee, why so mute?

Quit, quit for shame! This will not move;
This cannot take her.
If of herself she will not love,
Nothing can make her:
The devil take her!

Sir John Suckling

To His Coy Mistress

Had we but world enough, and time,
This coyness, Lady, were no crime.
We would sit down and think which way
To walk and pass our long love's day.
Thou by the Indian Ganges' side
Shouldst rubies find: I by the tide
Of Humber would complain. I would
Love you ten years before the Flood,
And you should, if you please, refuse
Till the conversion of the Jews.
My vegetable love should grow
Vaster than empires, and more slow;
An hundred years should go to praise
Thine eyes and on thy forehead gaze;
Two hundred to adore each breast,
But thirty thousand to the rest;
An age at least to every part,
And the last age should show your heart.
For, Lady, you deserve this state,
Nor would I love at lower rate.
But at my back I always hear
Time's wingèd chariot hurrying near;
And yonder all before us lie
Deserts of vast eternity.

Thy beauty shall no more be found,
Nor, in thy marble vault, shall sound
My echoing song: then worms shall try
That long preserved virginity,
And your quaint honour turn to dust,
And into ashes all my lust:
The grave's a fine and private place,
But none, I think, do there embrace.
Now therefore, while the youthful hue
Sits on thy skin like morning dew,
And while thy willing soul transpires
At every pore with instant fires,
Now let us sport us while we may,
And now, like amorous birds of prey,
Rather at once our time devour
Than languish in his slow-chapt power.
Let us roll all our strength and all
Our sweetness up into one ball,
And tear our pleasures with rough strife
Thorough the iron gates of life:
Thus, though we cannot make our sun
Stand still, yet we will make him run.

Andrew Marvell

Our Photograph

She played me false, but that's not why
I haven't quite forgiven Di,
Although I've tried:
This curl was hers, so brown, so bright,
She gave it me one blissful night,
And—more beside!

In photo we were grouped together;
She wore the darling hat and feather
That I adore;
In profile by her side I sat
Reading my poetry—but that
She'd heard before.

Why, after all, Di threw me over
I never knew, and can't discover,
Or even guess:
Maybe Smith's lyrics, she decided,
Were sweeter than the sweetest I did—
I acquiesce.

A week before their wedding-day
When Smith was called in haste away
To join the Staff,
Di gave to him, with tearful mien,
Our only photograph. I've seen
That photograph.

I've seen it in Smith's album-book!
Just think! her hat – her tender look,
Are now that brute's!
Before she gave it, off she cut
My body, head and lyrics, but
She was obliged, the little slut,
To leave my boots.

Frederick Locker-Lampson

A Thunderstorm in Town

She wore a new 'terra-cotta' dress,
And we stayed, because of the pelting storm,
Within the hansom's dry recess,
Though the horse had stopped; yea, motionless
We sat on, snug and warm.

Then the downpour ceased, to my sharp sad pain,
And the glass that had screened our forms before
Flew up, and out she sprang to her door:
I should have kissed her if the rain
Had lasted a minute more.

Thomas Hardy

Love's Philosophy

The fountains mingle with the river
And the rivers with the Ocean,
The winds of Heaven mix for ever
With a sweet emotion;
Nothing in the world is single;
All things by a law divine
In one spirit meet and mingle.
Why not I with thine? –

See the mountains kiss high Heaven
And the waves clasp one another;
No sister-flower would be forgiven
If it disdained its brother;
And the sunlight clasps the earth
And the moonbeams kiss the sea:
What is all this sweet work worth
If thou kiss not me?

Percy Bysshe Shelley

JUBILATION

The ring, so worn as you behold,
So thin, so pale, is yet of gold.
The passion such it was to prove:
Worn with life's care, love yet was love.

George Crabbe

From: The Fourth Booke of Ayres

There is a Garden in her face,
Where Roses and white Lillies grow;
A heav'nly paradise is that place,
Wherein all pleasant fruits do flow.
There Cherries grow, which none may buy
Till Cherry ripe themselves do cry.

Those Cherries fayrely do enclose
Of Orient Pearle a double row;
Which when her lovely laughter showes,
They look like Rose-buds fill'd with snow.
Yet them nor Peer nor Prince can buy,
Till Cherry ripe themselves do cry.

Her Eyes like Angels watch them still;
Her Brows like bended bowes do stand,
Threatening with piercing frowns to kill
All that attempt with eye or hand
Those sacred Cherries to come nigh,
Till Cherry ripe themselves do cry.

Thomas Campion

Song

Phillis is my only joy,
Faithless as the winds or seas;
Sometimes coming, sometimes coy,
Yet she never fails to please.
If with a frown
I am cast down,
Phillis smiling
And beguiling,
Makes me happier than before!

Though, alas, too late I find
Nothing can her fancy fix,
Yet the moment she is kind,
I forgive her all her tricks.
Which, though I see,
I can't get free;
She deceiving,
I believing;
What need lovers wish for more?

Sir Charles Sedley

The Sun Rising

Busy old fool, unruly Sun,
Why dost thou thus,
Through windows and through curtains call on us?
Must to thy motions lovers' seasons run?
Saucy pedantic wretch, go chide
Late school-boys, and sour 'prentices,
Go tell court-huntsmen that the King will ride,
Call country ants to harvest offices;
Love, all alike, no season knows, nor clime,
Nor hours, days, months, which are the rags of time.

Thy beams, so reverend and strong
Why shouldst thou think?
I could eclipse and cloud them with a wink,
But that I would not lose her sight so long:
If her eyes have not blinded thine,
Look, and tomorrow late tell me,
Whether both the Indias of spice and mine
Be where thou left'st them, or lie here with me.
Ask for those kings whom thou saw'st yesterday,
And thou shalt hear, 'All here in one bed lay.'

She's all States, and all Princes I;
Nothing else is.
Princes do but play us; compared to this,
All honour's mimic; all wealth alchemy.

Thou, Sun, art half as happy as we,
In that the world's contracted thus;
Thine age asks ease, and since thy duties be
To warm the world, that's done in warming us.
Shine here to us, and thou art everywhere;
This bed thy centre is, these walls thy sphere.

John Donne

Boldness in Love

Mark how the bashful morn, in vain
Courts the amorous marigold,
With sighing blasts, and weeping rain;
Yet she refuses to unfold.
But when the planet of the day,
Approacheth with his powerful ray,
Then she spreads, then she receives
His warmer beams into her virgin leaves.
So shalt thou thrive in love, fond boy;
If thy tears, and sighs discover
Thy grief, thou never shalt enjoy
The just reward of a bold lover:
But when with moving accents, thou
Shalt constant faith, and service vow,
Thy Celia shall receive those charms
With open ears, and with unfolded arms.

Thomas Carew

A Letter to Daphnis

This to the crown and blessing of my life,
The much loved husband of a happy wife;
To him whose constant passion found the art
To win a stubborn and ungrateful heart,
And to the world by tenderest proof discovers
They err, who say that husbands can't be lovers.
With such return of passion as is due,
Daphnis I love, Daphnis my thoughts pursue;
Daphnis my hopes and joys are bounded all in you.
Even I, for Daphnis' and my promise' sake,
What I in women censure, undertake.
But this from love, not vanity, proceeds;
You know who writes, and I who 'tis that reads.
Judge not my passion by my want of skill:
Many love well, though they express it ill;
And I your censure could with pleasure bear,
Would you but soon return, and speak it here.

Anne, Countess of Winchilsea

Never the Time and the Place

Never the time and the place
And the loved one all together!
This path—how soft to pace!
This May—what magic weather!
Where is the loved one's face?
In a dream that loved one's face meets mine,
But the house is narrow, the place is bleak
Where, outside, rain and wind combine
With a furtive ear, if I strive to speak,
With hostile eye at my flushing cheek,
With a malice that marks each word, each sign!
O enemy sly and serpentine,
Uncoil thee from the waking man!
Do I hold the Past
Thus firm and fast
Yet doubt if the Future hold I can?
This path so soft to pace shall lead
Thro' the magic of May to herself indeed!
Or narrow if needs the house must be,
Outside are the storms and strangers: we—
Oh, close, safe, warm sleep I and she,
—I and she!

Robert Browning

Romance

I will make you brooches and toys for your delight
Of bird-song at morning and star-shine at night.
I will make a palace fit for you and me,
Of green days in forests and blue days at sea.

I will make my kitchen, and you shall keep your room,
Where white flows the river and bright blows the broom,
And you shall wash your linen and keep your body white
In rainfall at morning and dewfall at night.

And this shall be for music when no one else is near,
The fine song for singing, the rare song to hear!
That only I remember, that only you admire,
Of the broad road that stretches and the roadside fire.

Robert Louis Stevenson

DESOLATION

April is in my mistress' face,
And July in her eyes hath place.
Within her bosom, a warm September;
But in her heart, a cold December.

Anon.

The Selfe Banished

It is not that I love you less
Than when before your feet I lay:
But to prevent the sad increase
Of hopeless love, I keep away.

In vain (alas) for everything
Which I have knowne belong to you,
Your Forme does to my Fancy bring,
And makes my old wounds bleed anew.

Who in the Spring from the new Sun,
Already had a Fever got,
Too late begins these shafts to shun,
Which Phoebus through his veines has shot.

Too late he would the pains assuage,
And to thick shadows does retire;
About with him he beares the rage,
And in his tainted blood the Fire.

But vow'd I have, and never must
Your banish'd servant trouble you;
For if I breake, you may mistrust
The vow I made to love you too.

Edmund Waller

Never Seek To Tell Thy Love

Never seek to tell thy love
Love that never told can be;
For the gentle wind does move
Silently, invisibly.

I told my love, I told my love,
I told her all my heart,
Trembling, cold, in ghastly fears—
Ah, she doth depart.

Soon as she was gone from me
A traveller came by
Silently, invisibly—
O, was no deny.

William Blake

Mary

It is the evening hour,
How silent all doth lie:
The hornèd moon she shows her face
In the river with the sky.
Prest by the path on which we pass,
The flaggy lake lies still as glass.

Spirit of her I love,
Whispering to me
Stores of sweet visions as I rove,
Here stop, and crop with me
Sweet flowers that in the still hour grew—
We'll take them home, nor shake off the bright dew.

Mary, or sweet spirit of thee,
As the bright sun shines to-morrow
Thy dark eyes these flowers shall see,
Gathered by me in sorrow,
In the still hour when my mind was free
To walk alone — yet wish I walked with thee.

John Clare

'Oh! that 'twere possible'

Oh! that 'twere possible,
After long grief and pain,
To find the arms of my true-love
Round me once again!

When I was wont to meet her
In the silent woody places
Of the land that gave me birth,
We stood tranced in long embraces,
Mixed with kisses sweeter, sweeter,
Than any thing on earth.

A shadow flits before me –
Not thou, but like to thee.
Ah God! that it were possible
For one short hour to see
The souls we loved, that they might tell us
What and where they be.

It leads me forth at evening,
It lightly winds and steals
In a cold white robe before me,
When all my spirit reels
At the shouts, the leagues of lights,
And the roaring of the wheels.

Half the night I waste in sighs,
In a wakeful doze I sorrow
For the hand, the lips, the eyes –
For the meeting of tomorrow,
The delight of happy laughter,
The delight of low replies.

Alfred, Lord Tennyson

Remembrance

Cold in the earth – and the deep snow piled above thee,
Far, far, removed, cold in the dreary grave!
Have I forgot, my only Love, to love thee,
Severed at last by Time's all-severing wave?

Now, when alone, do my thoughts no longer hover
Over the mountains, on that northern shore,
Resting their wings where heath and fern-leaves cover
That noble heart for ever, ever more?

Cold in the earth, and fifteen wild Decembers
From those brown hills have melted into spring:
Faithful, indeed, is the spirit that remembers
After such years of change and suffering!

Sweet Love of youth, forgive, if I forget thee,
While the world's tide is bearing me along;
Other desires and other hopes beset me,
Hopes which obscure, but cannot do thee wrong!

No later light has lightened up my heaven,
No second morn has ever shone for me;
All my life's bliss from thy dear life was given,
All my life's bliss is in the grave with thee.

Emily Brontë

Remember

Remember me when I am gone away,
Gone far away into the silent land;
When you can no more hold me by the hand,
Nor I half turn to go yet turning stay.
Remember me when no more day by day
You tell me of our future that you planned:
Only remember me; you understand
It will be late to counsel then or pray.
Yet if you should forget me for a while
And afterwards remember, do not grieve:
For if the darkness and corruption leave
A vestige of the thoughts that once I had,
Better by far you should forget and smile
Than that you should remember and be sad.

Christina Rossetti

Renouncement

I must not think of thee; and, tired yet strong,
I shun the thought that lurks in all delight —
The thought of thee — and in the blue Heaven's height,
And in the sweetest passage of a song.
O just beyond the fairest thoughts that throng
This breast, the thought of thee waits hidden yet bright;
But it must never, never come in sight;
I must stop short of thee the whole day long.
But when sleep comes to close each difficult day,
When night gives pause to the long watch I keep,
And all my bonds I needs must loose apart,
Must doff my will as raiment laid away, —
With the first dream that comes with the first sleep
I run, I run, I am gathered to thy heart.

Alice Meynell

'I have been faithful to thee, Cynara! in my fashion'

Last night ah, yesternight, betwixt her lips and mine
There fell thy shadow, Cynara! thy breath was shed
Upon my soul between the kisses and the wine,
And I was desolate and sick of an old passion,
Yea, I was desolate and bowed my head:
I have been faithful to thee, Cynara! in my fashion.

All night upon mine heart I felt her warm heart beat,
Night-long within mine arms in love and sleep she lay;
Surely the kisses of her bought red mouth were sweet;
But I was desolate and sick of an old passion,
When I awoke and found the dawn was gray:
I have been faithful to thee, Cynara! in my fashion.

I have forgot much, Cynara! gone with the wind,
Flung roses, roses riotously with the throng,
Dancing, to put thy pale, lost lilies out of mind;
But I was desolate and sick of an old passion,
Yea, all the time, because the dance was long:
I have been faithful to thee, Cynara! in my fashion.

I cried for madder music and for stronger wine,
But when the feast is finished and the lamps expire,
Then falls thy shadow, Cynara the night is thine;
And I am desolate and sick of an old passion,
Yea hungry for the lips of my desire:
I have been faithful to thee, Cynara in my fashion.

Ernest Dowson

INDEX OF POETS

REC. U.K. RET. PRICE £5.00